DATE DUE

SE 2 5 18			

DEMCO 38-296

The Last Samurai

An American Poem About Japanese Courage

by
James Sutton

1997 MELLEN POETRY PRIZE
Best Long Poem in Great Britain & the U.S.

The Last Samurai

An American Poem About Japanese Courage

by

James Sutton

Mellen Poetry Press
Lewiston•Queenston•Lampeter

THE LAST SAMURAI
An American Poem About Japanese Courage
ISBN 0-7734-2828-3

This book has been registered with The Library of Congress.

Author inquiries and orders:

Mellen Poetry Press
c/o The Edwin Mellen Press

Box 450
Lewiston, New York 14092

Printed in the United States of America

To the Honor of
Capt. Tameichi Hara,
the Last Samurai.

INTRODUCTION

This is fiction, an interview between an ex-admiral in the Imperial Japanese Navy and a captain in the U.S. Navy at the beginning of the Allied occupation of Japan, starring Toshiro Mifune and Harrison Ford.

Episodes were suggested by histories, biographies and confessions on both sides. Capt. Tameichi Hara leans pacifist, before the Bomb, when he decides that compulsory suicide betrays samurai values. In rejecting abuse of *bushido*, he's more samurai than the navy he serves. I was attracted by the irony of this and by his character. He is the last samurai.

This isn't his story, 'though it pays homage to it. This is what happens when events take on their own momentum, when bureaucracies are self-serving, when machines built to serve people require people to serve machines, when racism rules because we don't spend time with each other, when eyes are plugged with mud because light is painful – and nemesis that burns through mud when light can no longer be ignored. A time or place like any other, like our own.

Except for nuclear holocaust. *Difficult* to be lyric about this. Epic? The form glorifies war or condemns it. Prose? Too optimistic, even Hersey's *Hiroshima*, but especially Tolstoy's *War and Peace* – where peace beatifies because war cannot yet annihilate for all species. I chose dramatic monologue.

When sensibility changed after the Great War, Eliot went back a century to locate a form that could express the impossibility of creating meaning. He resurrected lyricism, more precisely its ghost. He chose it because prudery couldn't cope with public titillation of private sorrow. He was not "the Last Romantic."

Post-nuclear wasteland requires a form that can express our need to create meaning or perish. I go back a century for a form that can express the quandary of Hiroshima. I do this because lyricism can't cope with radioactive corpses. This doesn't make me "Neo-Victorian." Form follows feeling – or plays against it.

Sonnets play feeling at its most subjective against form at its most objective. When done well, the result is chords. Tennyson and Robert Browning create meaning through sound. This is a virtue among those who value wind instruments.

These sonnets were written between August 13 and August 26, 1996. They arrived whole, rhymed, alliterated, sprinkled with assonance, in sequence – with little editing. Despite the demands of their form, they're conversational. I enjoyed writing them, which improves the odds you'll enjoy reading them. Having something to say, they aim to create meaning.

Read aloud, their meaning changes as inflection incarnates things unseen. Poetry transforms in the act of remaking itself, as do poets and old warriors. The Last Samurai found forgiveness for such knowledge, by confiding it to a friend. I emulate him here.

— Saroyan's Birthday, 1996.

1945

I'll tell you, Captain, since you ask to know.
We took to fighting. Many people died –
so many that I can't recall their names. . . .
Because we two are friends, I won't deny
my part in it, or all the woes that came
from putting too much faith in what might be.
But you won't understand, unless you see
the *reasons* for the actions that we tried
and *why* we were compelled to ply the same
destructive waters, time and time again,
till vessels, men and ocean burst to flame.
We are an island people, bent for war.
     Unless you understand us, you won't know
     how mortal men could ever wreck things so.

My father gave me to another man.
Such was the custom in those times, to give
a child to someone childless that you loved.
And we were poor. He led me by the hand
and took me to his brother's house to live.
Ah, such a lovely place, set high above
our ocean city. When I saw the sea,
it seemed to stretch out from me, endlessly.
That is the part I liked – infinity.
Yes, I *was* lonely. They were kind to me,
my uncle and my foster family.
They helped me to become what I could be.
    My father took me there, obliged in part,
    but also to provide a better start.

The Last Samurai

Behind the house, down in a quiet dell,
among chrysanthemums along a brook,
I spent my brightest days creating boats.
I didn't know I'd sail them straight to Hell,
to temperatures where even glass would cook.
I go to school. The lessons all are rote.
So many signs to learn. It takes some time
to master thousands. Life was very strict.
The lesson, principally, was "get along."
This led to overlooking ugly times,
like cruelty against the poorly formed
or any who were different or were sick.

    We learn to numb ourselves and be the tool
    of others who are numb and also cruel.

I finish first, of course. "You're samurai,"
my fathers tell me, often. "We expect
this family to be restored through *you*."
So there I am, the youngest son of five,
now called upon to save us from our wreck.
Naive to think that samurai could do
as well again as they had done of old.
The gun, you see, blasted advantages
that discipline had clenched in simpler times.
"You will be excellent," they said; so I was bold.
They never understood the damages
that come from having constantly to shine.

> Of course I loved them all. They sacrificed
> so I alone could live a better life.

About this time, my foster father died.
He calls me to his bed and says to me,
"Always remember: You're a samurai.
So be prepared at any time to die,
but never *seek* your death. Too easily
bushido is betrayed by those who try
to sink to martyrdom, instead of sail
against a storm to reach their port of call.
So do your best. Be always on your guard.
Increase your effort, so you will not fail.
But don't believe the final goal of all
is dying easy. Living on is hard."

    With that, he puts his sword across my knees
    and slowly gives my hand a final squeeze.

I finish grammar school. But where to go?
I need some more, but more is far away,
and we are poor. I hear my brothers say,
"We'll help out with expenses" to my dad.
Each is a farmer. Each gives what he had.
You can't repay a debt like that, you know.
I do my best to pass the entrance test
and find myself admitted, one of five.
For days, I was the proudest son alive.
I had enrolled *our* name among the best.
I graduate up high, although the rest
were also gifted; make the "top ten" list.
     But once again, I'm dragged down by the stuff
     that weighs us down when best is not enough.

I ought to tell you *why* we were so poor.
It wasn't merely that our plot of land
was just an acre. Such a tiny farm
could not sustain us, 'though my parent's hands
were hard as rocks from trying. No, the harm
flowed from our history, when sinecures
were ceded to the Emperor by their lords,
who, up to then, held title and estate.
No samurai were needed, after then,
to fight in battles or administrate.
Some wander through the land as homeless men,
or knowing just one craft, as bandit hoards.

> My grandfather was lucky. He got land,
> but not enough to prosper once again.

I had three choices: Army, Navy, none.
A public education was required,
since there was no more money – not enough
for private education. I had one,
and only one, *real* chance to make it higher:
to pass the entrance test. And it was tough.
Which one to try? The Army or the Navy?
I try for both, since either chance is slim.
Some try for years to pass. But they had time
that I could not afford. Just *once*, for me,
and failing that, my future hopes go dim.
I hop a train. The Army quiz goes fine.
    I have no trouble zipping through the test.
    I thought I passed, but like the Navy best.

Why this should be will not seem strange to you.
A naval officer should know the way
the sea can beckon – how on tropic days
the sky turns green at sunset, just before
the sun dips as it drowns in waves once more.
You know the tricks that sea and fog can do,
the sudden danger when you hear the surf
or *fail* to hear as sand flies in your face.
A dicey problem that. Or how you steer
against a raging sea for all you're worth
to keep a wave from rolling up your trace
and pooping you so quick you disappear.
　　　I know, of course, such things aren't new to you.
　　　I heard of that typhoon your fleet went through.

Then, too, my city squats against the sea.
It beat the bloody Mongols off the coast,
creating our *first* Navy. After that,
ours are the men who row off eagerly.
Raiding the Chinese mainland, our proud boast
is *"We're* not here to die." We soon grow fat
with juicy treasure our wags carry home,
and this goes on for *centuries.* Alone,
we made those who attacked us wail and moan.
Many a Chinese dynasty succumbed
because it *dared* to threaten. Sailors hum
as Ming and other dynasties go mum.
    So I was influenced by this and knew
    where I could find great things for me to do.

I go to Eta Jima for the test
and take a room inside a small hotel –
the wrong one, as it happens, since the room
abutting next to mine contains a bed
that fills my ears with groaning. Seems the maid
was quick to offer favors. As for mine,
she seemed the sweetest girl I'd ever seen.
I hadn't talked to many. Well, I fell.
I fell in love, I mean. A blushing groom
too shy to seek advantage. Precious Jade –
a lovely name – gives me a little sign.
"Yes, I could love you, too." So two young teens
    sit talking through the night; and when dawn came,
    I go, exhausted, to take tests again.

After the test, I travel home to wait.
Anxious, I wait for days, and days, and days;
but nothing happens. "Army life for me,"
I tell myself. "Our Navy's never late,"
but late they were. I didn't know their ways!
It took ten days for their telegraphy
to reach my doorstep. Tearing open slow,
I tap the envelope to look inside,
but pass it to my dad so he could see.
"It looks like Navy life is what will be."
I never felt so happy, so alive.
"Banzai!" I shout, as I prepare to go.
       I didn't know, from this day on to that,
       I'd never see my father or go back.

"The Island" was a terror. We were trained
by being badly beaten. *Any* lapse
would get a plebe a dozen in his face.
And when he got them, each in his platoon
would get one for his error. Interest waned.
I saw too many friends cringe and collapse.
We lost initiative. What a disgrace,
to brutalize the best and brightest, too.
I tell you, Captain, we were punched apart.
The lesson was, "Obey, and don't make waves."
Training like that was fatal from the start.
For those who gave me beatings in those days,
    I never tried too hard. I made salute
    as I was taught, obediently and mute.

Four years of this would crack the bravest heart,
and mine was close to breaking. Things at home
were getting worse and worse. My father died.
My sister left her husband. Lived apart!
A thing unheard of. Women live alone?
She must have had a reason. So I tried
to modulate the broken world I lived in
against the breaking world I'd left behind.
I had to make my *own* way. *That* I knew.
Yet I resolved that I would never give in
to those who did no more than stand in line.
Yes, living *is* the harder thing to do.

     I finish in the top third of my class.

     I could have done much better than just pass.

Time wasn't fully wasted. I made friends
and also learned some English. Later on,
this proved the wisest thing I could have done.
But at that moment, senior Navy men
weren't certain how to shove my hat along.
"He isn't *right* for us; in fact, he's *wrong*."
Oh, I was samurai; but I was poor
and from a place they laughed at, "from the sticks" –
as you once told me you were. I pressed on,
but I could see my chances growing fewer.
No battleship for me. I'd take my licks
in some low-glory billet or be gone.

    A square head soon decides that I should be
    consigned to submarines eternally.

That didn't put me off. I love the sea,
and it's far more relaxing underneath –
much smoother there, much more *cam'raderie.*
I was the best torpedo man around.
This "highest rating" pleased me, endlessly.
A hot torpedo, in its metal sheath,
is just as deadly as a fish could be.
I guess you know, by now, that ours were sound,
not like the ones *you* had that wouldn't fire.
Yours bumped their way inside and teetered there.
They sent me two to study. Lovely gyres,
but all for nothing. You had duds to spare.

    And just a twelve-mile range! But ours would go
    for twenty miles and travel fast or slow.

At the Academy, throughout my time,
I posted letters to my Precious Jade –
great, wide adoring letters, hopelessly.
To meet a woman was a major crime.
You'd think my love for her would start to fade,
but it grew stronger. Younger men can be
seduced by love for someone they can't see.
But writing back, she shows her fire for me.
I love her for those letters. No one hides
between the lines of writing. What's inside
sticks out its neck. A turtle swimming free
is how she seemed to bare her soul to me.

    At graduation, when I looked her up,
    I learn a man can't love his first enough.

As I was rising, she was rising, too.
Instead of chambermaid in some hotel,
she greets me as a geisha in a gown.
You Westerners don't understand this well.
A geisha isn't sex that can be hired;
she's just a hostess, there to keep things gay.
She has a choice, to go or else to stay.
They're trained and *talented.* To be desired
and make *you* feel desired: the geisha's way.
At first, I go to see her where she works,
but I can't swing the charges on *my* pay.
She has me take a room, and like a jerk,
        I let her book it. Didn't understand
        she went in debt to take me by the hand.

We don't talk of emotion. Island men
are taciturn, keep feelings to themselves.
But you will understand me, Captain, when
I tell you that I love her more than wealth
or power, glory, even more than self.
That's what love *is*. You understand me, then.
The seven kinds of love consist of this:
of loving someone more than loving self.
You open *up* your self and take the risk
of reputation, pain and even health.
You think that island men don't get lovesick?
Well, you can put *that* notion on the shelf.

     I love her more than I love *family*.
     I never thought a love like *that* could be.

While loving in a train and in a car
and in chrysanthemums where no one goes;
while loving by a stream and on the beach
and places where a guest takes off his shoes;
while loving for the letters that she wrote
and for the way she always made me feel;
while loving for the way I came to dote
on every word, since every word was real;
while loving for the music in her hands
and how she answered, deep between her knees;
while loving for the way I was her man
and she was mine forever, endlessly,

    I had no thought that love itself would be
    the reason love would end for her and me.

My captain calls me in. "Are you aware
you have a geisha paying off your bills?"
Of course I wasn't. "She's gone into debt
to pay the charges on that room you share.
Two thousand yen. I hope you've had your fill
of conduct unbecoming. Swabs get wet
when they go into town. We all do that.
But you can't go on doing what you like.
Her boss has written me. Of course he's *right*.
You can't receive while adding to her lack.
So tell me *your* decision. Please decide."
I tell him that I'll marry her tonight.

    "Marry a *geisha*? No! Resign. You're through."
    The trouble was he said it to her, too.

He keeps me at the base and hard confined.
I soon receive a letter. "I can't be
the reason all your hopes will be destroyed.
I love you far too much.   I am resigned
to going far away where I won't see
you're loving face again." I have no choice,
because her love is more than love of self.
The trouble is I feel the self-same way.
Cold numbness overtakes me. "Let me die."
Yes, suicide, because that's how I felt.
But living on *is* harder. Every day
announces one more pang. Too numb to cry,
     I stare at the abyss till I go sane
     and learn I'd never love that way again.

They send me to destroyers after that.
A good torpedo man is hard to find.
They rate me with the best. They also thought
submàriners could help the bigger hats
get poor destroyer tactics into line.
But gunnery's the billet that I got!
You've got to wonder, sometimes, *if* they think.
A gun is tricky, even little guns.
It soon warms up and sends its volley high.
There's so much math. We had to shoot at night.
I learn a way to mute the glare that stuns,
throwing you from your timing as you blink.
    Soon I was hitting targets. Adding rates,
    I get promoted – mostly slow and late.

When last we went to war, we beat the Russians.
A simple time, because we caught them sleeping.
I wish we hadn't, seeing, after that,
we thought we could defeat the Brits *and* Prussians.
Invincibility was slowly creeping
up every camisole, down each cravat.
Meanwhile, at sea, a gun of mine blows up.
A piece of shrapnel rips my finger off.
It made me seem much braver than I was.
I was just standing there. I hear a pop,
but never feel a thing. Then something hot
concusses near my head. I hear it buzz.

     It made me understand, that day to this,
     that life or death is mostly hit or miss.

Some square head pulled my card, because he saw
that I spoke English. Ordered on my way,
I'm sent to roam your land with diplomats.
I do some spying, but no more than you!
I just keep both eyes open. "Attaché"
means hanging out with stuffy bureaucrats.
Amazing what you hear at those receptions,
what you can see just traveling up and down.
You let us tour, if we showed you *our* ground.
A courtesy for courtesy. Deception
controlled our "time between the wars." I found
the few ships you were building very sound.

     I also thought I'd never live to see
     a nation such as yours our enemy.

You had ten times the people that we had;
strategic industries, where we had none.
You lagged behind, but you could quickly build.
There was real spirit in your sprawling land.
I was amazed at all the things you'd done,
the dams you poured, the faces in those hills.
We had no raw materials, no oil.
I knew what fleets of submarines could do.
There was no need to make you enemies.
You were, like us, anti-colonial.
But as an island people, what we knew
about our neighbors left us all at sea.
    Too bad we didn't spend *time* with each other.
    We might have learned to call each other brother.

Well, you and *I* spend time. We ship around
and see the sights together. We write memos
on each other, reading each one's mind.
Remember when we went to Puget Sound?
I played at poker with so fierce a tempo
no one could tell when I was bluffing blind!
I did a lot of gambling, even then;
and even more before, at Naval school.
I got so good I sent big money home.
It was a treat to beat the senior men.
How dare they think we junior men were fools!
I shuffled for revenge, mostly alone.

    "Don't win," my friends say; "You'll become a goner."
    But I was safe. It was a debt of honor.

They send a square head over to help out
and wire him telegrams in Naval code.
This means he has to have the code around.
He keeps it by his side, always about,
inside a leather briefcase. On the road,
I'm not sure what he did. One time I found
he'd hopped a train to somewhere, to Dubuque.
There's no destroyers there! It was a girl
he'd taken up with, snug in some hotel.
A perfect place for spies take a look
as he was being pleasured in a whirl
they'd manufactured, to evoke a spell.
     I wonder now when he went on the road
     whether he compromised our Naval Code.

A navy man should know the role of booze. . . .
We serve it on our ships. I know *you* don't;
only *your* Navy muddles on this way. . . .
Perhaps you think a snort will make you snooze!
Unless it's politics from those who won't. . . .
The Brits pass out a ration every day.
It *can* get out of hand, but just ashore; . . .
we have a custom of returning toasts.
A man comes up to you, gives you his cup;
you drain it, wash it, fill it, give him more. . . .
Another one comes up, if you're the host.
A samurai will rarely say, "Enough."
    The secret is – I hope you won't claim foul –
    a cup of oil makes booze pass through the bowel.

While sailing back, I'm asked to make a stop.
"Drop off at Pearl, and take a look around.
Report on dispositions by the bay.
Take pictures, sketches." I was never caught.
My strategy was simple: "Take high ground."
I took my lunch and dinner every day
in restaurants that served our native fare
above the harbor. Looking down from there,
I check off gun positions. Everywhere,
this was routine. The world was still at peace;
but all the Powers were spying, just to see
if others were abiding by the Treaty.
        It was a lovely post, the best I'd known.
        I did my work, played poker and went home.

I don't suppose it matters if I share
my observations of your naval state.
Your S-class submarines were small, *too* small
for the Pacific. Your torpedoes, fair,
but not approaching ours in size at all.
I saw another thing that sealed our fate:
The aircraft that you had weren't very good.
I made report, and it was passed around.
This figured in our thinking later on.
No one could see how fast your men would scoot
beyond production models on the ground
to new design, unknown and far along.
    I guess we were defeated, finally,
    by your inventiveness, not enmity.

'Though we *deserved* your bitter enmity,
the way the war got started – suddenly.
That's not the way that it was *meant* to be.
You were to get a notice, in advance.
We had no wish to look uncivilized
or stir a hornet's nest. A bad mistake.
Some square head, missing how long it would take,
sent people home. When messages arrived,
one code machine was left. This happenstance
left typing understaffed. Our Embassy
sent *home* the hands required to act in time,
missing its deadline. Someone cut too fine.
      It went about the worst that it could go.
      Only a telegram would be more slow.

But you, as well, deserve *our* enmity.
Why did you spring your final grievous fault?
Didn't you understand what would transpire
by setting an embargo on the sea?
An island people takes that as assault.
That was the match that kindled fatal fire.
(Of course it wasn't right, not morally
or militarily, for us to chase
a Chinese general into China's heart.
That was no place for island folk to be.
Wrong *time* to fight a war. Wrong *war*, wrong *place*.
The Army was at fault, right from the start.)
    Unless you understood and said, "Let's go,"
    because your President was in the know.

We let our hearts grow harder in those years.
We thought the Treaties made us second-class.
You seemed to take the major powers' part.
You did things that confirmed us in these fears.
You, too, confined us to the brutal past –
when immigration laws kept us apart;
when gunboats told us what we had to do;
when troops enforced concessions gained by force;
when opium was sent to pacify;
when what we owned was taken, shipped to you.
It's not a pretty picture. Race, of course,
reduces men to items of supply.

      Your part in all of this was very small;
      but you were backing Europe, after all.

We had good men who didn't want to fight.
They understood your country was too strong –
including Yamamoto, who had thought
that war with you could never turn out right.
But *politics* led him to couch it wrong:
"For six months, if we give it *all* we've got,
I'll give you victories; but after that,
I *cannot* give you any guarantee."
He meant, "Win in six months, or else we *lose.*"
This was interpreted, by other hats,
"Be more aggressive now, for victory."
He didn't offer facts so we could choose.

> Our eyes were clogged with mud. No one could see
> how we were mired in our machinery.

I had my doubts, and they were honest doubts.
How could we fight along four fronts at once?
Did we need Pearl as well as Philippines?
Need we do more than push the Dutchman out?
I drop in on my Admiral, playing dunce.
"I know that staff work isn't done by me.
I'm just a low torpedo man. And yet,
I wonder if there's more than we can chew."
He looks at me and says, "I think so, too;
and many others, also, share your view.
But I'm afraid there's nothing *we* can do.
The time line is contingent, but it's *set*.

  And you're our *best* torpedo man!" I smiled.
  A compliment goes far, once in a while.

I'll tell you of my part, since you're my friend,
'though I've no wish to speak of it again.
A veteran would rather let dogs lie.
I've seen too much to bark like other men
astride a bone of bravery, in a den.
I've seen the eyes of good men who have died.
Dead faces, too, have stories they can tell.
I try to shy away from bloody facts
and don't speak of my losses. But I'll speak,
because you ask to know. I'll tell you well
what fact resides in this, what truth in that,
just as I knew it. Is this what you seek?
    No wonder that you've asked me to your nook,
    seeing you've been assigned to write a book!

They bounce me back to submarines. Okay,
and doubly so, for I was in command.
A lowly billet, but I call the shots.
I'm ordered out to Pearl, to join the raid.
I'm wasted in a skirmish line that day,
achieving nothing. Old square-headed men
think submarines are there to make it hot
for any ships pursuing. Snares were laid,
so we became a rope instead of lances.
We could have looked for tankers, lain in wait,
or searched for carriers that fatal date;
but we were squandered in defensive stances.
     Alone, I could have rounded Tierra del Fuego
     or in a pack, just strangled San Diego.

Nagumo led the raid that shocked the world.
I got to write it up at his debriefing.
Nagumo lays out how he blasted Pearl.
I write it up the same way he is speaking,
but it was clear his judgment wasn't right.
A *single* wave of 'planes. *No* follow up.
The tankfarm and the subpens left *intact.*
Nagumo should have sent his fighters *back.*
He wasn't *up* for more aggressive stuff.
Maybe he'd been awake too long that night,
or else it shows the weakness of our training.
"Nothing ventured, nothing gained" means *straining.*

    Nagumo: "Nothing ventured, nothing lost."
    He didn't stick his neck out, at our cost.

Throughout this time, I'm working on a thesis.
"The way we fire torpedoes is all *wrong*.
The *math* is wrong, at least for our destroyers."
I point this out, as happy as a rhesus.
The answer had been waiting all along.
Amusing how it rattled those sea-lawyers.
What's harder for old hats than brand-new doctrine?
Too much invested with the old to change.
"But I have *proof* – in higher mathematics."
The old rule has us firing in an action
in ways that make us miss at *any* range
along an arc. "We *have* to change our tactics."
        Their answer is, "You'll join the general staff."
        They'd kept me out, but I was in, at last.

When I say "kept me out," I mean just that.
Assignment there was by examination.
I study and do well, but nothing happens.
The nobly born inherit braided hats.
So in frustration, out of desperation,
I think, "If I could get their doctrine sharpened,
they'd *have* to take me in to learn it *from* me."
And that's the way it happens. But there's more.
After I teach them and they all agree
that what I'm telling them has *got* to be,
they bounce me from their castle by the shore
to captain a destroyer far at sea.
    The message was, "We keep our good minds close.
    We think it's fair to keep you off the coast."

I know you won't believe it. Number One:
for sheer prestige and honor, General Staff.
And Number Two was battleships, of course.
Destroyers next. Then submarines. And last
came naval aviation. What they'd done
was turn things upside down! The best on shore,
the worst up in the air, the rest at sea.
The very picture of a *peacetime* Navy,
trying to keep things calm instead of hot.
But combat makes its *own* reality.
You've got to *win* to get the meat and gravy.
In battle, politics ain't *worth* a lot.

>   The peacetime give-and-take we take for skill,
>   when done in war, will often get you killed.

By now I had a wife. Here's how it happened.
I read an ad and laughed until I fell.
"Please, wanted: naval husband. Write me now."
I thought its craziness was just back-slapping.
It seemed an invitation straight from hell.
It wasn't that at all, I learned. And how.
I passed it to Intelligence and said,
"Is this a spy?" An answer soon came back!
"Regarding inquiry concerning spy,
no blame attaches to this lady's head.
Her widowed mother wants a naval lad
because she has to share her daughter's life
    and thinks a man who sails upon the sea
    won't be home much to trouble girl or she.

"Regarding girl, a knock out, very sweet,
well-trained in all old-fashioned ways to serve.
Regarding mother, very, very rich;
late father owning downtown property
in Tokyo, Kyoto. Lovely feet.
Unlikely her great loyalty will swerve."
"This time as good as any to get hitched,"
I write my brother. He makes inquiry.
They check me out, and soon we have a meeting.
Things take off after that, and I'm not sorry.
Takato was the one that I'd been seeking,
a haven from the grind of war and glory.

> Her mother's happy, too. I wasn't there!
> But I get back. We had twin girls, a pair.

It didn't take much brains to do the math.
"You have 4x destroyers to our one.
Each one of ours must sink 4x of yours
and not be sunk itself." Unlikely path,
more likely to undo us than get done.
But now, we were committed to this war,
so I commence to whip up my resolve.
"I'll work to get my four and not be sunk.
I won't be caught off guard; I won't be stupid.
You won't catch *me* in port beside a wall,
torpedoed by a sub while in my bunk
or bombed to pieces." Danger makes me lucid.
    But many others had to drink the sea,
    for being less aware than they should be.

There was a moment when I drowned with shame.
I have a tanker on the ropes and burning.
The crew pulls off in boats; and as I'm watching,
a rating opens up and starts in shooting.
There was no need for that. They were unarmed.
"Cease fire," I call at once; but men are dead –
machine-gunned to a man. One had no arms.
I pull away, a blot on my good name.
I couldn't do much more than to report it.
No punishment for anyone who did it.
They'd have asked *me*, "Say, what's inside *your* head?
No prisoners," the square heads all were saying.

   "Gun discipline," I said and sent men tripping.
   This was the first time that I saw us slipping.

I often wonder hard about our codes.
That floosie from Dubuque is on my mind.
Also co-incidence. I'd get a flash that said,
"Make rendezvous at such-and-such an hour;"
and I'd get there and find a submarine,
an air patrol, some other enemy.
And not just once; it happened all the time.
I tell you, things like that don't make you bold.
And if you're not, before too long you're dead.
So I respond with boldness and with power.
I get my vessel early to the scene
and try to get the *other* guy to flee.
    I send a memo up. Some square head said,
    "You're crazy. Codes like ours cannot be read."

That was the feeling, "victory disease."
We were invincible, but not aware.
Most beaten nations seem to feel that way –
at the beginning. Persia on the seas.
Bismark and Hitler. Madmen everywhere:
Napoleon; Crusaders, in their day.
Inferiority, if you ask me,
seems to present as bluster. It's complex.
Excuse my pun. I don't mean to excuse
by making light of things that shouldn't be:
A sailor *has* to see, or he gets wrecked.
But when he's taken in by his *own* ruse,

> he wrecks *himself.* By choosing *not* to see,
> leaders confuse what *is* with what *should* be.

Before too long, we spot a submarine.
My lookout sees it first and far away.
Someone has lit a cigarette on deck.
A match gleams in the dark, lighting the scene.
A hundred men die for a smoke that day.
I call for battle speed, begin the trek
to get in range before the sub goes down.
"Make turns for thirty knots, set every charge."
Then making ready with my larger guns,
I send her to the bottom of the sound
with just three salvos. Oil-filled like a barge,
she burns up like a match. "That sub's all done."
     Right after that, I give up all my smoking.
     No need for me to risk our lives by toking.

My men start cheering. What an ugly course.
There is no joy in killing men for me.
"Remember, men are *dying* over there.
No need for you to shout until you're hoarse.
In fact, I think the better way would be
for all of us to stop and say a prayer.
These men were sailors, just like you and me.
They died for country; therefore, happily."
That put a damper on festivity.
No need for celebration *I* could see.
It could have been *us* just as easily,
condemned by one small cigarette from *me*.

    And so, we say a prayer most solemnly,
    before I thank the lookout in his tree.

The Last Samurai

A naval battle often is confused –
especially a battle using guns.
You know the odds: Just two per cent are hits.
Ships go this way and that. Men are bemused.
The winner, mostly, is the bolder one.
It's hard to win on defense. Who forgets
the fall of naval gunfire? If they live.
There's nothing like it. Shells as big as cars
go whizzing till they drop. "Don't fall on me!" –
a feeling any samurai forgives
once he has felt projectiles hit afar
and wonders, next time, if he'll cease to be.
    You hear a roar, an echo just as terse.
    I knew that men would think up something worse.

About this time, I get myself a leave.
It isn't long. I ask my brother up.
He asks me, "Do you think we'll win the war?"
I pull him close, grabbing him by his sleeve.
"This little island can't *produce* enough.
The Allies outproduce us more and more.
So far we've won, as they've done more things wrong;
but don't expect their ignorance to last.
They are a clever people. They learn fast,
and they are brave. Yes, just as brave as us.
I fear the coming year will treat us rough,
and after that, worse things will come along."
    He had no thought at all that we could lose.
    A propaganda mill ignores bad news.

They couldn't hide the raid on Tokyo.
"B-25s attacking from the sea!"
It *has* to be a carrier, although
your radio says they came from Shangri-La.
This was repeated. Many looked it up
and couldn't *find* it. "How far could it be?"
my XO asks me. I say, "Very far."
The 'papers call this raid "mad useless stuff"
and claim that "every 'plane has been shot down."
That wasn't likely. Bombing served an end,
diverting air armadas all around
to keep it all from happening again.

     How in the world could anyone believe
     reports of our invincibility?

The Last Samurai

I'm off to Midway. *Nothing* there goes right.
We go in thinking nothing could go wrong.
No one should under-rate the force of luck,
but it was character that lost that fight
and indecision. Square heads bounced along
from one blow to another and were sunk.
We even changed our rules during war games.
When those defending "sank" some carriers,
we plucked them from the deep and then played on –
as if, out there, our fleet could do the same!
No one objected. Loyal terriers.
Our chance to learn from error soon was gone.

> The gods must laugh. They give us signs to see,
> and we ignore them. Omens come to be.

Our battleships lie useless after that.
In fact, since Pearl, they hadn't budged from port.
Our submarines get squandered, once again.
A skirmish line at Midway's what I had.
A submarine that lingers can get caught.
Detected by patrolling ship or 'plane,
a line of submarines can be destroyed
in series down the row, *because* they wait.
In fact, this happened later. Was it chance?
Easy to do, if you were reading codes.
The worst at Midway was our loss of 'planes.
A lack of crews forced a defensive stance.

> We couldn't train them fast enough to fight
> or train them well enough to do it right.

Bad patterns get established. "Split your force.
Lead off with several feints. Commit ships piecemeal.
Engage at sea like mounted cavalry,
and stake the race on how the *other* horse
is going to run." Such tactics were unreal,
without a link to what goals *ought* to be.
Every omelette the Staff tries to hatch
starts off with a willing American rooster!
We grabbed feathers once, only at Leyte.
Halsey was Halsey. *He* wasn't hard to catch.
"Ride to the sound of the guns." A Custer booster.
But try this every time? The staff was crazy.
        No, *that's* not it. The staff refused to *see*.
        They never doubted "final victory."

I'm sent to do some missions down the Slot.
The fact we're there at all explains a lot.
Our fleet was somewhere else! Our troops go in
and quickly get ground up. We send in more,
and *they* get wiped. A square head, safe ashore,
discovers, at that rate, we'll never win.
"REQUIRED DO UTMOST NOW TO RESUPPLY."
An island where we never should have been!
Our fleet was still intact. We could have tried
much earlier, before our ranks were thinned,
to get troops out or bolster up our side.
I can't help thinking of those misused men.

    The big hat, Yamamoto, was to blame.
    He made the same mistakes over again.

Some thirty other ships with me are sunk,
so I become a marvel: "Captain Luck."
Of course it's more than that. I stay aware
and steer away from all the standard junk,
by-passing all the predigested truck.
I put my faith in being really *there*.
I *use* my eyes. Attending what I heard,
I don't lie to myself. I don't pretend.
It's not a method often used out there.
In fact, few leaders use it *any*where.
"We break because we are unused to bending."
Eyes plugged with mud make *any* choice absurd.
    I'll tell you, Captain, how *I* stayed alive.
    I never, ever, did the same thing twice.

And then, the glory part. I sink three ships –
and one a cruiser – all within an hour.
Fifteen of them against fourteen of us.
It was a melee. Sudden fire and hits.
All fog and darkness, and we had no radar.
My new torpedo theory raised a fuss.
I prove it on a hyperbolic run.
Ships loom up in the night, and some are friends.
More than a few shoot wrongly at each other.
We lose hydraulic steering; then we're done.
So we abscond, back to our base again.
We take repairs among those we call brothers.
    I make mistakes, but somehow we survive.
    I was a hero, glad to be alive.

There was a price. There *always* is a price.
Four dozen of my men were lying dead,
and some in pieces. Lost my good XO.
If I had turned away (as he advised)
not giving rescue, he'd still have his head.
We never found his body. I don't know
why people think that war is full of glory.
It's eyes of friends agape among the dead.
We had to bury them before first light.
We couldn't let them lie another night.
I come down from the bridge and wash his head.
I wrap him in my coat and tell his story.
    Among the guard of honor in a line,
     not one dry eye – including also mine.

Thirty-five holes, all bigger than a meter.
Five more where one-inch shells fail to explode.
A dud torpedo, hanging out the side.
Hydraulic fluid, less than half a liter.
Nothing at all inside the sonar node.
The sheerest luck that *any* were alive.
Repairs would keep me beached for sixty days.
Your side could fix it up in less than ten.
We didn't have the *means* to fight with you.
The harbor master does what he can do,
ordering parts, not knowing if or when.
The bay we ran for, Truk, is where we stay.
    But it's now risky dropping anchor there.
    You had achieved supremacy of air.

So I fly home. My brother's house was robbed.
My twins weren't getting food enough to eat.
Your submarines were strangling us. The sea,
our oldest friend, is now our enemy.
Without the sea, an island smells defeat.
You seemed to pick out tankers to get stopped.
Your silent fish had found their voice at last,
as I predicted. Easy wins were past.
I eulogize the dead to those at home.
I tell my wife. "I doubt that I'll be back."
Her mother tells me, "Live." My heart goes slack.
Small comfort grief was never mine alone.
    There never was much comfort, peace or rest
    for those who rode the Tokyo Express.

I fall into my bed and try to sleep.
Amazing all the things my poor ship did.
Day in, day out, all night, for near two years.
But it caught up with me. I set my cheek
to pillow two whole weeks. Not that I hid.
Fatigue from battle, not collapse from fear.
Two years of fighting; others lasted *one*.
That fact *alone* should rate some kind of rest.
It wasn't long enough. Classmates come by.
They've heard about the battles that I've won
and came to pay respects. The very best
asked me about new tactics that I tried.

    It isn't long before square-headed men
    decide that I should put to sea again.

A broken-down division's what I got,
a brace of ships that no one else had tamed.
My job was "Get these old four-stackers trained."
And yet, I really can't complain a lot.
To get command paid honor to our name.
And anyway, I'd get to sea again.
I hop a train and take a look around.
Reservists and inepts, nothing but thumbs.
"I think you'll like the challenge," my boss said.
I toured the ships. "They don't look very sound;
They're much too slow on their torpedo runs."
I felt misused, because I'd been misled.

    But I resolve that my four ships will be
    the best destroyers in the whole damn'd Navy.

I take no pleasure as I criticize.
Most of the men I chide were kind to me:
Kondo and Yamamoto, and Nagumo.
I don't *like* cutting giants down to size;
but giants put their feet down carelessly.
So please believe me when I say to you
I wasn't angered by what happened next.
I take my four destroyers out to Truk,
and Kondo takes *three* of my ships away!
By right, I should have been *little* vexed.
I'd taken this command, and I was *stuck*.
My ships were redeployed that very day.
     A promise made in war can go awry.
     I make the best of it and say, "Aye, aye."

So Kondo says, "You're beached at least three months.
You'll train your ship and also read reports."
This means that I've become his General Staff!
My job becomes to schedule several runs
to ferry soldiers from that foul retort
where they lay dying. Too late, by a half.
The radio calls this pull out "victory."
"*Tenshin*," I said – "advancing to the rear,"
with sixteen thousand rotting in the muck,
twelve thousand more to steal away by sea.
When I got there, they couldn't even cheer;
they were too hungry. I sail back to Truk.

     I read reports about the Bismark Sea.
     "Skip bombing, radar." Not a victory.

It isn't hard to see the reason why.
As usual, we do the same again;
but much has changed. You have control of air.
Good things, six months before, that we had tried
now bring disaster. I retrain my men.
Alone, I put to sea and teach them there.
I work them hard and set my standards high.
"You need *perfection* when your life's at stake."
They didn't understand when I got mad
and bawled them out. "Stand by; another try.
You've got to get it *right*. The risk you take
when you do something wrong is that you *die*."

  In just three months, they get a training year.
  They really weren't as bad as I had feared.

How could we think you'd *always* take the bait,
that same old bait, and always play *our* game?
But that's just what we *did.* "That's it; enough.
Why don't we try to hit them where they ain't?
Permission, Sir, to tell the Chief the same."
"Okay," he says. "*You* go and quack such stuff."
He didn't think I'd *go* to High Command,
but that's just what I did. I went to see
the second in command, the Deputy,
to schedule time to visit the Old Man.
When I arrive, his orderly seems chilly.
Perhaps his boss thinks coming here is silly.

　　　I pass into his room and bow my head.
　　　Both he and Yamamoto lie there dead.

P-38s had splashed them as they toured.
That happens when you lose control of air.
It also happens with a broken code.
I write up my concerns, now reassured
they'd get a hearing. "They should be more fair
because of this disaster." So I showed
no understanding, really, of their minds.
They squint into my light, look at its beam;
contrast, examine, cough to say their piece,
and then conclude raw guts are doing fine!
They didn't see the polyp that I'd seen.
Useless to push ahead. I had to cease.

    "The C-in-C," they said, "bears major blame.
    Despite the risk, he flew on just the same."

I'm loved and hated. Isn't that the way?
"I'll make them pull together like a crew.
They've got to *fight* together, like one man."
I didn't want to be there on a day
when someone did what someone shouldn't do
and killed us all. Therefore, I took a stand.
"You'll work all seven days till things are right."
The captain of my ship takes strong exception.
"Don't they deserve a bit of rest and fun?
Couldn't they see a movie just tonight?"
No, they could not, because of my perception
work must continue till all work is done.

     By right, this choice was his alone to make.
     But he agrees with me, for safety's sake.

We ship out for Rabaul. That's where the rest
of my four-stackers waited in the bay.
During detachment, one had found success.
"If one could win, the rest might meet the test."
They'd gone to sea as I came on my way.
I waited like a fledgling in a nest.
Then word came back, "Two of your ships are sunk."
Your offense grew much faster than our defense.
"Your third ship's hard aground. It, too, is lost."
Why did it happen? "Navigation stunk."
As for their quality, I make no pretense
that carelessness could sail without a cost.

     The bright side was my crew began to see
     why I demanded training ceaselessly.

So *we* become replacements. I am told,
"Continue your ships' mission when they sank."
Same route, same time, same cargo, everything.
Incredible? Insane. Risk every man!
We could have sent your side a telegram,
since there'd be no surprise. Our "planning" stank.
"Why, for a *third* time, do it all *again?*
And in the *same* way, too?" Where were their brains?
I spoke up at the briefing. *That* was bold.
Mostly we smiled and never said a *thing.*
"Change? No, impossible. It's all been *planned.*
Except, please sail up front and take the van."
        A clever ploy. I drop it in a hole
        when I stand up again and tell him, "No."

Inferior commanders waste their men.
Frontal attack is stupid. Banzai charge
just throws away the force that's there to fight,
since every one of ours has to kill ten
and stay alive. That's why I dared to barge
my big nose in that meeting. "That's not right."
I owe this to my crew. "My ship is *old*.
A new *fast* ship is needed up ahead."
I say it loud. Their whispers criticize,
"That man is too persistent and too bold."
The very things we need to stay alive!
"Why should we wish to multiply our dead?"
     I win my point. I didn't have to sail
     in front. I thought the mission bound to fail.

Douglas MacArthur. What a brilliant mind.
He realized, with air supremacy,
he could let strong points wither "on the vine."
He overturns old dogma, instantly.
That is the training of a samurai.
"If one would hit you low, then hit him high;
if one would hit you high, then hit him low."
A thing we samurai once got to know:
Just hit 'em where they ain't. "*Never* go back
to where the foe expects you, to the track
you've beaten down once, twice or three times past."
When sailors don't react, their ships don't last.

     Four ships get told to do it one more time,
     steam up a narrow channel in a line.

"'Planes have been sighted." We keep sailing on.
"Same course, same speed." We rush on to our doom.
Slow as it is, my ship falls off behind.
"Go now to overboost?" my X-O said.
"No, battle stations." So we sail along.
Black hulks loom up. "Attention. Turn to port.
Firing torpedoes." Our side doesn't move!
"Full starboard!" Yank torpedoes have us *caught*.
A minute for the wheel to take its head.
"*Now* go to overboost!" We steam for room.
The other ships are gone. "Where could they be?"
I hear explosions, far across the sea.

     Also a thunk, somewhere along the stern.
     I wonder if *my* ship is next to burn.

I have two-hundred fifty troops on deck,
a hundred drums high-octane gasoline
and am outnumbered, maybe eight to one,
but I come back to see what can be done.
"Look for survivors." It's a hellish scene.
Your gunfire inches closer to our necks.
I witness fire, explosions of a kind
not many could survive. "They're gone, all three."
I radio back to base, to get instructions.
Those at the base are of a different mind.
"Come back," they say, "the fastest way by sea."
So I make smoke and try to foil detection.
  The marksmanship was perfect from your cutters,
  even the dud that went clean through my rudder.

War has its small rewards. As they are leaving
the troops, who'd spent two days between our decks,
run down the gangplank, form up carefully,
turn to my ship and then bow gracefully.
They know how close they came to being wrecked!
As for my crew, they have no cause for grieving.
They did a splendid job. I grant them leave,
the first time-off they had. "You earned it, men."
And then I have a thought. "Where is the lookout?"
I call him to the bridge. "Roll up your sleeve.
I bought this in New York. You take it then.
Without you, we'd be paddling in a dugout."

    The man's astonished he's received a gift.
    Sometimes you have to give your crew a lift.

They come back bloody from their night ashore.
I call the lookout. "Well, what happened, man?"
"We all got drunk," he says; "I show the crowd
the watch you gave me. Someone says, 'What for?
Just for retreating?' Bad things happen then.
Someone yells 'coward', and he yells it loud.
Our crew stands up, just like a single man,
and after that, the place just flies apart.
I didn't lose your watch, 'though. Here it is."
I post them all to sickbay, since their stand
has left them battered. Also rich at heart.
Up to this point, morale was hit and miss.

    But after this, I notice something new:
    A clump of men has turned into a crew.

Staff learns a lesson. Doctrine starts to change.
No longer are we asked to take on fuel
and work as transports. "Let's not look for duels,"
I tell my CO. "We are, in the main,
responsible for those we're here to guard.
Let's *nurse* these transports, make *sure* they get through.
If *we* get sunk, then don't *they* get sunk, too?"
I tell my staff, "Don't lean on doctrine hard.
Adapt yourself to what you find at hand.
Be cautious, too. Don't toss your lives away
from carelessness. Live for another day."
"And keep on training hard," I tell each man.

I thought I'd gotten through. At least I tried.
It's worth a little sweat to stay alive.

We go to sea again, another run
protecting barges. "'Planes, up in the moon."
We call in ours, to see what can be done.
They radio back, "Destroyers, closing soon."
We try to lure them off. They follow us,
believing we're still loaded up with troops,
but we've changed tactics. Soon they make a fuss
to reach our transports. So we make a loop
and come at *them*. Torpedoes hiss and break,
but no one scores a hit. "One premature,"
exploding as it crossed a vessel's wake.
Our CO, then observing, calls it sure.

    "We got a cruiser." I saw none that day.
    He got a medal. We just got away.

We got away again, a second time.
Two missions with no damage. That was rare,
and no one calls us cowards who was there.
The other side has radar. What a crime
to send good ships to battle almost blind.
Your radar changed my tactics. "We can't close
inside 3,000 meters, at the most."
This was the best solution I could find.
We go on two more missions and are lucky.
Again we go unscathed. We lead the way
for battered cripples sailing up the bay.
My crew and I are feeling bright and plucky.
    We have a nickname now, and it was catching.
    "The Indestructible." My crew was meshing.

Another mission. "Sighted by a 'plane."
It flies away, returns and flies away.
"Nothing." So we stand down, to break the strain.
Then out of nowhere, hell breaks loose again.
"Dive bombers. General quarters," I bark out.
"Turn left full rudder." Bombs go off abeam.
"Get me flank speed, with overboost, right *now*."
My XO flinches, seemingly in doubt.
He's never heard me call for that much steam.
Fuel *flames* up through our stack. It's quite a show.
The radio room reports, "Sir, from the 'plane.
He thinks he's *sunk* us. 'Going home again.'"
    This time, *I* cheer. We finish up the trip.
    Thanks to the engine room, we saved our ship.

An overboost can be a risky thing.
It takes a quarter-hour to kick a ship
out of its doldrums up to highest speed,
even at flank. The strain makes turbines sing
or even bends them. At our breakneck clip,
we might have caused some damage in our need;
so we're inspected. *"This* tub is *unfit.*
Your engine's *wrecked.* Even your rudder's holed.
All your machines require recalibration.
The barnacles on you are one-inch thick.
No remedy. You'll have to make for *home."*
The crew objects! "Sir, It's discrimination.
    Can't you do something? Our men want to fight!"
    That's when I knew that they'd turned out all right.

I needed downtime. Rest, I needed rest.
A worn-out man *can't* think of stuff that's new.
Rest keeps a crew from breaking. Also me.
After so many months, I couldn't sleep
unless I drank a liter of good booze.
Going cold turkey, I became a pest –
irritable, excited. Just a heap.
I couldn't sleep, or if by chance I did,
I'd start perspiring. Nightmares claw my brain.
I'd wake up screaming, in a burning sea.
But two weeks later, I'm on top of it.
So I go back, prepared to meet the strain
  that comes from fighting with no hope of gain
  and knowing that you won't see home again.

I gird my loins and march back to my men.
The war, the war. We're back at sea again.
Another melee. Each side loses one,
but I sink one and damage one with guns.
The barges all get through, so we succeed.
We make mistakes. Your side makes even more,
so we escape again, without a scratch.
I wonder what your side would ever do
if we attempted doing something new.
Mentioned in dispatch, "*You* do what we *need*.
You get your troops and barges onto shore."
So I'm sent off to fetch *another* batch.

    The C-in-C commends all those on board
    and solemnly presents me with sword.

So my CO regales us with a party.
But I got ugly. I got up and said,
"Please tell me why our big ships lie at Truk.
Will carriers no longer go to sea?
Why do destroyers have to bear the weight
of every push that goes on in this sector?"
And I continue, swaying as I hector.
"I am content to bear this dismal fate,
but for my men, I wonder what will be.
My ship survives, but only through rare luck.
When this runs out, we also shall be dead."
He offers me a cup, which I drink hearty.

> "Here, take this sword. I'd rather have, I think,
> enough good *sake* for my men to drink."

The bombing started then, without a break.
Rabaul is now a risky place to be.
I have three ships. Soon we go out to sea.
Another transport mission. Then, at dawn,
we find ourselves with bombers all around.
"Break on your own." I didn't hesitate.
We all get home. Then we go out again.
At Bougainville, we re-enforce our men.
Another operation doomed to fail.
"If Bougainville should fall, our homeland falls."
I thought it likely. Later, on the trail,
we spot a column, battleships and all.

    We send our barges scuttling to the rear
    and look for trouble. I could *smell* it near.

We stupidly take bait and play your game.
Dumb to accept this battle of attrition.
Our admiral, raised for his noble name,
had never fought a battle. His precision
left much to be desired when making turns.
Two ships collide. Big shells came tumbling in.
First salvo. "Hits!" A cruiser starts to burn.
"Radar controlled." Confusion grabs our men.
Our columns *cross!* We almost crash *four* ships.
Another's hit. "Come in and give us aid."
"We must decline." He's straddled, end to tip.
I won't repeat the error I once made –
  four dozen men I'd lost to save a few.
  I pull away. Our ship has work to do.

My XO was incensed. "They've called us *in*.
That's our CO. We have to follow *orders*."
I shut him up. "There's no way we can win.
We can't save those, and we could lose these others.
Port helm!" I said. "Full speed ahead! Attack!
Those are your orders. *Find* the enemy
and *close* with him. Rescue is always *last*."
I leave our cruiser burning on the sea.
In the ensuing action, I shell two
and sink a third as I go running by.
We make for home again, one of the few
unscathed by convolutions on our side.
      Imagine still demanding tight formations
      after a year of tintinnabulation.

The cruiser's crew is rescued by a sub.
It finds our CO small, broken and weak:
"Excuse me, please, for breaking under pressure."
I hear the engines groaning on my tub.
I've run an hour, full speed, at hide-and-seek.
My other ships get back, much to my pleasure,
but I don't make report. I have a hunch
an air raid will come down. We wait, prepared.
A hundred 'planes roar in, just after lunch.
Directly for the harbor's mouth we steer.
They come in low and fly into our guns!
We shoot down five, before this raid is done.

> Just as before, none of my ships is hit.
> With this success, I feel relieved a bit.

I go ashore, to see the C-in-C.
"Here's my report on what I've seen today,
the battle at Empress Augusta Bay
and also my emergency sortie."
To my surprise, the Chief agrees with me.
"You were correct to leave the cruiser there,
since it was under concentrated fire.
The fight is where a fighting ship should be."
But then he dressed me down with one long stare.
"Just one more thing remains that I require.
I think you ought to have these thirty yen
so you can buy some *sake* for your men."
    And then he laughs. The word had got around
    that I had thrown his sword upon the ground.

Reconnaissance was bad. Then it got worse.
We lost a fleet of cruisers at Rabaul.
They'd been sequestered there, over a year.
They'd never put to sea! Your fleet comes near.
We see no carriers. Our spotter's fooled.
Our pilots' information was a curse.
Again, I make emergency sortie
and get my three ships safely from the bay,
the only three that do. When I return,
I see nine heavies, all completely burned,
including seven cruisers. In a way,
this was "Pearl Harbor" payback from your fleet.
    Complacence bred disaster yet once more,
    as at Malalag Bay, two years before.

Our 'planes go out to find your fleet at sea.
I hear reports of sinkings. Hard for me
to credit these reports. "These claims are high
for 'planes well known to misidentify.
Why don't we ask them all to verify?"
The answer was, "We'd only frustrate men
who are already working hard to try
to realize the good reports they sent."
Perverse philosophy, because it meant
it was okay to cheapen those who *could*
for swabs achieving *nothing* as they went.
I didn't think *bad* claims were very good.
      The losing side often can't see things clear.
      Those who lose nothing often pay too dear.

My engines couldn't take it any more.
Then we get orders back to homeland shores,
but we don't go directly. We get asked
to "drop some freighters off, as you sail past."
It sounded like a milk run. What a horror!
Both air attack *and* submarines. I *lose* one,
the only time I lose a transport ship
entrusted my command. As for the terror
of air attack, one moment I feel stunned.
The next, raw danger clears my head a bit.
"Skip bombing! Engines, go full speed ahead!"
My navigator: "Zig-zag?" "No, *ahead!*"

  As we go straight, the bombs bounce overhead.
  So once again, quick thinking saves our heads.

The base commander seems preoccupied.
"Rabaul has just been bombed. . . . The toll is high."
I start to make report on what I've learned.
He doesn't seem to hear, although I try
to follow him direct to the latrine.
Like Meneläus, dazed. "So many burned. . . .
I've only first reports. . . . I don't know why. . . .
Oh, by the way, your orders home are green. . . .
Your ship is too beat up to hang around. . . .
You sail next week, . . . as escort for two cruisers, . . .
assuming you can keep up with those bruisers. . . .
I gather that your engines still are sound."
         "Well, I can make two dozen knots or near,"
         but can't report good tactics purchased dear.

We make it home, directly into dry dock.
As engineers strip barnacles away,
they find the rudder *holed*. Right in the lock,
reporters get together for a field day.
Within a week, those rascals make us heroes.
"How these *brave* men survived, without a loss
of man or ship by guns, 'planes or torpedoes. . . ."
As if we'd done this service at no cost.
The finest place in town throws us a party.
Twelve geishas come to serve us, all for free.
I get there early. Not a man is tardy.
Our home port gives us hospitality.

> The finest gift that my men could receive
> I grant them later, thirty-two days leave.

The trouble was they all came by to *see* me.
They tell Takato, "*Please* don't be displeased.
We've gone through *hell* with him in southern seas.
It's *right* to pay him tribute at his knees,
even if we lose time with families,
because he pulled us *through*. Without his skill,
we'd all be carcasses; we'd all be dead."
They pass the cup around, with hearty will.
It was the worst leave that I ever had,
the wettest one at least. Oh, I was pleased,
to hear them buzzing 'round my house like bees.
"Here's to our safety, luck, celebrity."

But it reminded me what we'd been through
and made me wonder what more we could do.

The war keeps going badly. Fire control
and radar are reducing many ships
with single volleys. Many ships are old
and get more obsolete on every trip.
We have few pilots, or we have few 'planes.
Without air cover, bigger ships just hid.
We try to catch up, but we never did.
At home, the shelves are empty. Submarines.
Children are quiet, hunger on their lips.
The 'papers call for victory. "Be bold!"
The pages of our lives begin to rip.
This is what comes from doing what you're told
     only, without *attending* what you hear.
     Silence *creates* a holocaust of fear.

I'm transferred from my ship – beached high and dry,
again by orders of the High Command.
"Your orders are that you shall teach a school
and share the tactics you were first to try."
As if this were a fault. "To save your men,
you've innovated, time and time again.
Therefore, your Navy calls on you to teach
every torpedo man that you can reach."
I file a protest, once again the fool.
They wanted me, and that was that. "Too bad
you have to leave our ship." My boys were sad,
broke discipline to wave to me. What lads!

    I saw them crying as I pulled away.
    I go back home and cry alone that day.

My XO comes to see me. "Sir, I'm here
for several reasons. All of them are good,
but none of them is formal. I'm so full
my feelings may betray me into tears.
You saved my life. You taught me what to do
and patiently. I acted like a mule.
I even questioned orders. You were kind
despite the many worries on your mind.
Despite all this, you recommended me
to take your place among the men you'd trained.
The feelings now within me churn so deep
it's hard for me to bow or even stand.
        Sir, I salute you. Till we rearrive,
        I'll do my best to keep your men alive."

I get new orders. "Build torpedo boats."
They want the kind that you had all along.
"And train good crews to keep these boats afloat."
My men are *air* reservists. Right or wrong,
this program was too little and too late.
The *fastest* boat did only twenty-five.
Engines were culled from *airplanes*. What a fate
to serve in them. Their crews would sink and die.
They *weren't* torpedo boats; they were just *scows*.
"We built a battleship that stunned the world.
Now we can't build an *engine!*" I said low.
I hear retort that makes my nostrils curl.
    "It doesn't matter. Just enjoy the ride.
    Command sends heroes home so they'll survive."

To my first class of graduating men,
attending exercises for this feat,
I gave this speech. "You're heading straight for *hell*.
Without *great* effort, you will know *defeat*.
Your boats are *slow*. They *don't* run fast and well.
The enemy's are *better*. Hiding, then,
you'll have to strike from stealth, then run and *hide*.
Avoid all duels inviting your attrition.
Use hit-and-run, as I have tried to teach you.
Stay off your radio. Keep low smoke emission.
Use camouflage. Whatever else you do,
don't think that victory is on your side.
    You're target practice if you *once* forget."
    I heard the High Command was much upset.

Within a week, my former ship was sunk.
An air attack had battered it at Truk.
My XO had been sleeping in his bunk.
Despite his training, that poor man got stuck.
Our C-in-C was drowned in a typhoon,
the very storm your fleet went scrambling through.
He was replaced by someone from the moon.
The High Command selected someone new
with *no* experience of war at sea,
a man unknown to *any* at the front.
I had to ask, "What can their thinking be?"
I catch hell for my graduation stunt:

> They send me to the sticks to run a new
> torpedo training base. My home town, too.

The Marianas Turkey Shoot. Saipan.
Nagumo dead. The list goes on and on.
Throughout this time, I think about my men.
"Only a month before their lives are gone."
My orders turn to *kamikaze* then.
"Prepare now to defend our nation's shores."
Just what had I been *doing?* "Train your men
for one-way ramming. As the war
requires frogmen to walk beds of the sea
and detonate explosives with their hands,
prepare men for this combat role to be."
But this was suicide, for all my men!

     Was there a way to bring them some relief?
     I thought about it, and my thought was "peace."

You've got to wonder if I was insane.
Imagine going to see *your* President
around Command, to tell him what *you* thought.
The Emperor. I'd do it all again,
for *any* chance to save so many men.
I'd never met him, since we all were taught
he was a god, divine and not like us.
I wasn't sure he'd even let me in.
But I went up, with papers in a knot,
in full-dress uniform. Get in or bust.
My thinking was, if *he* could understand,
there'd be a *chance* for peace. I ask for him.

    To my surprise, I get in as I sought.
    "Oh, what a fix I've got me in," I thought.

They pass me to his study, filled with books.
His Majesty is sorting butterflies.
I start things off by bowing. When I look,
I see "the lineage that never dies."
I stand there, silent. He looks up at me
and breaks the ice. "So beautiful, you see."
I don't know what to say. But I begin,
"I've come to see you, Sir, about my men.
But may I ask you why you've let me in?"
"So few come here, except the ones they send."
I understand then. *No* one is in charge.
A state has no more steering than a barge!

  The Army, Navy drifted as they would.
  Nothing was organized for doing good.

"Your Majesty, Japan has *lost* the war.
We have to find a way to end it *now*,
or else we lose the flower of our men
as England did, back in the war before.
We'll need them, after this, no matter how
we have to compromise to make an end."
I told him of the errors that we made,
which we repeated, never learning much.
I told him of command that didn't know
a day of combat and the price we paid.
"Even without complacency and such,
there was no way to win, right from the go."
     I tell him all of that. He said, "I see"
     and pointed out a bug. "A real beauty."

He seemed a gentle man, a caring man,
a man who really *wanted* to do right.
But he was overwhelmed by trouble then,
even as I. Sadly, I bow goodnight.
When I get home, I write a little haiku,
this: "See the Emperor/ *in* his Palace, a
butterfly/ trapped in amber." Sad, but true.
"Maybe I should resign, with malice a-
forethought."   But what would *this* do for my men?
"They *must* have leadership, or else *no* chance."
I trundle back to base, attacking then
the lack of virtue in this happenstance:
     "They order suicide and call it honor.
     That's not *bushido*. Overboost disorder."

We pay the penalty, if we should fail.
But we're not ordered to it. We're *obliged*.
We aren't obliged to die without a chance.
New doctrine was *official* suicide.
So I resolve to take a daring stance.
"Each one of you is free to choose his nail,"
I tell my men assembled. Then I said,
"Each one will have a choice. Here are the three:
the boats; the one-way boats; the frogmen team.
No one is asked to sacrifice his head.
No questions asked. Each one of you is free
to act as you think best, just as it seems.

     My single wish is that you come and tell me.
     My office will be open till three-thirty."

I didn't think that things could get much worse.
Of course they did. New orders hit the deck.
"We have a further tactic to rehearse.
Let men ride on torpedoes, as they wreck
all of the vessels shortly to invade."
Now that was madness. How could they hold *on?*
Some fifty knots our fast torpedoes made.
Hadn't they ever *seen* one hiss along?
The frogmen's gear they sent us was a joke.
The regulators jammed, so men got sick.
One strafing, and the PTs cracked and broke.
With luck, one *might* get in a single lick.
    Then finally, we get an even shake.
    "STAND BY UNTIL THE BIG INVASION BREAKS."

And then a strange thing happens. Suddenly,
Captains are smiling, when saluting me.
"What's going on?" I ask the Base CO.
"Congratulations from His Majesty."
"What's this about?" "I swear that I don't know.
But I suspect you'll hear about it, though."
He hands me cold chrysanthemums to wear,
insignia for my tunic. "What? Oh, no.
So now *I* am the square head." "So it seems.
His Majesty has asked that 'you should bear
responsibility for what you know.'
That's what it says. I don't know what it means.
      But this has been endorsed right up the line."
      His Majesty does deadpan humor fine.

We go on waiting. Nothing much goes on.
I doubt we could have given you a fight.
No oil, no 'planes, bad food, too few good men
who knew what they were doing. In the end,
we'd have been bringing bamboo sticks along
to fight you in the countryside, at night.
It might have gone a week. Still, we hung on.
Paralysis, without the will to act,
results from incapacity to see.
Why did we keep on fighting, uselessly?
None would be *first* to get the dying done.
Maybe we'd *never* have our future back.
        Square heads decide the fleet should go to sea.
        Off Okinawa, big ships cease to be.

A young lieutenant comes to me and says,
"Please, Sir, I need permission to be wed
and you're my final hope." This lad might die
without a chance to wiggle from this mess.
Why not some happiness before he's dead?
Better than numbness after tear-stained eyes.
But I go through *all* the formalities.
"The lady, is she from good family?"
"The lady is a geisha, Sir. I love her."
I wonder if he saw my feelings stir.
"Does she, by any chance, have any debt?"
"Not that I know of, Sir. I pay the rent."
  I give permission to a happy man,
  and he's so pleased he asks me to attend!

"I have no father, Sir. No family.
They're all dead in the war. Neither does she."
"I'll do the honors, then," I told the lad.
"We'll use my uncle's house up in the hills.
I haven't been there since I was a boy."
I was elated, if a trifle mad.
"At least you two won't have to pay more bills."
He starts to protest, so I try a ploy:
"Allow me, please. It's something I *should* do.
Won't you reciprocate the way I feel?
Come, please agree." He tries, once, to renew
his mild objection. Then our bargain's sealed.
    "If you will set the date and let me know,
    I'll make arrangements. But please don't be slow!"

The day is set. We drive into the hills
and chant the wedding in a quiet glen.
Among chrysanthemums, two take their vows.
It's early in the morning. Quiet. Still.
The bride is beautiful. I tell her then,
as we're together under one great bough,
"I knew a woman like you, long ago.
Her name was Precious Jade." "Oh, I know her.
She *works* with me. I asked her to attend
and told her how kind *you'd* been. 'I *can't* go.'
She *cried* after I asked. She was *disturbed*
she couldn't be here. What a lady. Men
        attend *her*, rather than she wait on them.
        I'd *like* to be like her. I don't know when."

A blinding flash. A sudden wave of heat.
A little later, rumbling like a train –
immensely louder. Great concussive shock.
After a time, the ground leaps at our feet.
"The ammo dump's gone up!" I try to gain
some vantage point and set out for the top,
but find a raging cloud – half-pink, half-black.
Then it gets dark, and I can't see a thing.
I stumble to the grove. "What's this about?"
For twenty minutes, we sit in the *dark*.
"What's happening?" But none of us can bring
a shred of reason in, to work things out.

     And then, one thing begins to seem too clear:
     My family and men are under there.

I still can't see the sun, but I get going.
"I must return to base," I say to them;
"I've got to go, to see what I can do."
I didn't know what I'd be driving through.
"Sorry to leave you, ladies, in this glen.
We'll join up later, where we all are staying."
So I drive down, and what I'm seeing stuns.
From far away, I see whole hectares leveled.
The city *churns* with flame. And something strange:
Street poles are charred and leaning, every one.
Also, ceramic tiles containing bubbles.
Things get much worse as I reduce the range.

    Dead horses in the streets. Horribly blind
    inchoate people, burned out of their minds.

The strangest thing was shadows, human forms
etched into bridges, also granite walls.
I couldn't understand it. Then I saw.
"These are remains of *people,* now all gone."
Shadows of substance, turned into a pall!
The sight and thought of that put me in awe.
"What kind of weapon *does* a thing like that?
It *has* to be a weapon," I believed.
Then I recalled what Akakatsu said,
"No, we can't build one; that's the honest fact.
But they can't either." I had felt relieved.
But he had been half-right. So many dead!
    So there was only one thing it could be:
    A bomb made from atomic energy.

"I've got to reach my base," first thought of all.
My house was on the way; we lived nearby.
I look for signs of my own neighborhood,
but I can't find a thing. Then I recall
a standing pipe nearby. I make a try
to find the intersection where it stood.
It's bent, but standing. Then I find my home.
There's nothing there. It's just a burned out lot.
So is the school. My wife went to the bank.
It's farther in. I realize they're gone.
There's something metal, something small and hot
half-buried in the ground. *That's* when I sank.

     I recognize the shape. Turns out to be
     chrysanthemum insignia. . . . Please, excuse me.

I finish off my crying and drive on.
It wasn't wise to drive much farther in
because of radiation. All are gone –
except a few who are no longer men,
just burnt-out hulks of flesh who'd soon be dead.
I turn my car around, start heading out.
I wasn't sure just *what* I was about.
"Fate catches up to you," as someone said,
"when least expected." As I drive around,
I see a woman all alone. Her face,
horribly burned, is staring at the ground.
Despite all that, my heart begins to race.
    I recognize her only by her eyes.
    It was my Precious Jade, to my surprise.

Her clothes had saved her. Wrapped in cummerbunds
some distance from the heat, she has survived.
Light colors help, although her clothes are burned.
I feel too much to speak. We are alive.
Of all my thoughts, this is the only one
that seems to matter. As her wits return,
she looks at me and tries to run away.
Her face is that disfigured. Thirty years
of being in command come into play.
"Get in the car," I tell her. "No more tears.
Living on is the harder thing to do."
She looks at me and nods, knowing it true.
      Then we drive to the hospital to see
      what could be done for her, and our city.

You shouldn't think that I forgot my duty.
The Red Cross Hospital is where I go
to figure out what's happened. Those still left
would put in there for treatment, or to know
whether a loved one were alive or dead.
Of course I went to save a woman's beauty.
But no demerits; I worked on the same.
I ferried seven wounded as I went,
then gave my car up as an ambulance.
We were among the first to reach the entrance.
That was a break. We go to where we're sent,
lucky and early. Soon, too many came
    to justify attention to a face
    too burned to seem part of the human race.

My home town's named "broad island." It's a delta:
six islands cut by branches of a river.
Think of a flatiron pointing toward the sea
pressed into mountains. That's how it would be.
Most houses – made of wood, built helter-skelter –
burned out completely, leaving not a sliver
every eight years or so. Fires were expected.
The blast, arriving early in the morning
upset *hibachi* all across the town.
Even beyond the blast zone, fires *connected*.
A single bomber, *after* all-clear warnings.
Toward hypocenter, nothing could be found.

    Two hundred fifty thousand, in our core.
    About as many soldiers, back from war.

Of course it *was* a military base –
soldiers and sailors; also some munitions –
but nothing major. Just one plant for steel
and two for making rayon. My decision
is "move as many out as can be wheeled
to one of them." This had to be the case.
The Red Cross Hospital was just too small.
All this was done without authority,
absent a government. No power left.
Small groups or single people did it all.
Amazing how we did what had to be
without direction, orders or the rest.

     Moments of crisis, truly, seem to be
     when we become ourselves with clarity.

I talk to people, listen to their stories:
"A single bomber." People just ignored it,
as they were told. They just continued working.
Farmers in fields, and city folk commuting.
"It's the rush hour." People moving *toward* it,
out in the open. *Purposefully* gory.
Children at school. The bank was not yet open,
women outside. "Four airplane engines straining."
A high-g turn. "Two parachutes appearing;
a blinding flash." Confusion and mass groping.
"A wave of heat." Flesh, hair and clothing burning
or simply disappearing. "Hell is here."
　　Some burn up in the heat caused by the blast.
　　A firestorm comes along and burns the rest.

We get a little help, with none to spare.
The background radiation's not that high,
just ten times normal underneath the blast
and three times normal just a throw from there.
Perhaps not many people have to die
from radiation, silent death that lasts.
There seems to be a "hot spot" like a ridge.
We call it "fallout," dust motes from the Cloud.
Triangulation shows exactly where
the weapon turned our city to a shroud.
We find "ground zero," measuring to there
from shadows flashed on walls and on the bridge.
    Later, I mention blast height to your team.
    "That's classified!" the leading square head screams.

When you consider what this blast had meant –
how wax of deafness melted and was gone;
how mud of blindness dried and blew away;
how angry pride, once gushing, had been spent –
notice that we *still* sinned. "We've done no wrong;
we did just what we *had* to." In one day,
atonement, expiation, cleansing fire
expunge responsibility. *No guilt,*
no shame. We play the *victim – to* the *hilt!*
The blast just *redirects* our base desires.
We are not purified by fire at all,
but feed the same aggression that brought downfall.
 Watch out for island people, bent for war.
 By means of trade, we'll rise to fight once more.

The web that holds our lives gets swept away,
along with our whole city, on a wind
that carries us in flames to . . . expiation?
So one could hope. Except it wasn't so.
We still required another demonstration
before we were prepared to let war go.
An ill wind, to be sure. Had *no* good been?
Was there not *one* "just person" in Its way
that could have turned the wrathful Hand away?
Were we *so* wicked *cities* had to die?
Does it make any difference, anyway?
What meaning *is* there, but within each eye?
    There was *no* meaning in It. *We* create
    such meaning as we *can*. Such is man's fate.

That's what I learn from that. And from the war,
this little fact: "Nothing's *as* subversive
as *doing* what you're *hired* for." Even *if*
survival's at stake. Boring at the core
of what you're up to; being assertive
other than for effect; teaching the stiff
how to weave and swivel; doing your best
when no one's looking, fails to endear you
to those who wish to gain the point they seek
rather than climb an unexpected peak
higher than Niitaka. There's a few
who set their course with honor. But the rest
    just sail on blindly till it's far too late.
    One's character is finally one's fate.

What happened next may seem bizarre to you.
There seemed no meaning for me anywhere.
Eternal Verities I'd served with pride
were fused to glass by fires burning inside.
I'd seen too many die, too many stares.
Then I decide there's something I can *do*.
I take up Precious Jade and march away.
We beg outside the Palace, to atone.
"Forgive me for the ills I didn't stop."
My uniform, without chrysanthemums,
embarrasses the passers-by, who gawk.
Your soldiers come and drive me off one day.

    So I start begging outside your Tribunal.
    No one, as yet, has asked for my removal.

It's not from lack of money that I beg.
Tako's endowment pays me, even now
when there's so precious little one can buy.
I beg on principle – imagine that –
for gaping eyes that stare among the dead;
for open sores that scar a woman's face;
for diplomats and cowards, in disgrace;
for eyes and ears that fail their hands and heads.
"Behold my beggar's bowl" – my Admiral's hat!
"Remember that we *sinned*." That's what I cry,
or else I fire *this* grapeshot at the bows
of those who won't acknowledge what I said,
"Refuse to look? Craven square-head men!"
I scream out after them, "Never again!"

So Jade and I go begging at the Square.
She sits on this side; I sit over there.
She gets more money. People see her face.
They look at me and think I'm a disgrace –
which is my purpose. "Think of what we did
and *didn't* do. Think of the truth we *hid*."
So I sit watching square heads, day by day:
Your square heads moving quickly, making way;
our square heads moving slowly, some to die –
should the Tribunal's list so certify.
And why *not* die, because of what was done
or wasn't done? Or just because you *won?*

   As for this "Court of Justice," all I saw
   was further machinations of the Law.

Well, who *is* guilty? Is it just the man
who carries out bad orders? Or just he
who passed them on? Or maybe just the one
who had the lives of others in his hand
till trapped by circumstance, he comes to be
another victim of wrongs that were done?
What of the men machine-gunned by my ship?
Was *I* responsible? I was in charge,
but gave no order; and I moved to stop it.
What was *my* blame? Should I have moved more quick?
Punished the gunner, primed for sudden discharge?
And I was *there.* It's vain now to retalk it.

    We're all war's victims. Let us change our ways.
    "Sometimes you're worse than us," I think, some days.

Consider those who ordered *down* the Bomb –
your President, *his* Cabinet, *his* staff.
Did he *believe* "a million troops will die."
An estimate *that* large is surely *wrong.*
Timing the drop with Yalta makes me laugh.
Does he believe the *Russians* will turn shy?
He doesn't *know* the Russians. Once again,
you make the error that you made with us.
Diplomacy is not an ultimatum.
No good can come of that. They, too, are men
willing to die and turn themselves to dust
rather than live in fear and desperation.

     Consider, too, they're beat up pretty bad.
     Courage is all those Russian "comrades" have.

What of the men who made or flew the Bomb?
Are they so blameless, just because they won?
Their kind of weapon surely qualifies
for "crimes against humanity." It's wrong
to wipe out cities. Half a *million* gone.
Your bomb count is too low. I certify
our camps were swelled with soldiers back from war –
as many as were living back in town.
Children at school, women going to banks.
You killed them all. *Indiscriminate* gore.
But square heads, on *our* side and also *yours,*
still say okay to that. I say, "No, thanks."

    You suffer from the same disease as we.
    Leaders say, "Yes," when they refuse to see.

I could go on, sneak out the easy way –
make everyone to blame. Or be more subtle,
say "The big machines we built to save
wound up destroying us, making us slaves
in servitude to freedom." Or claim *muddle*,
saying, "It can't be *known*." Or lean on Fate,
or what's *behind* Fate – character only –
controlling where we go and what we choose,
or fail to choose. Or lay it all on Chaos:
"Randomness itself selects the payoff."
Or "More than we could handle of the new."
Or "Ancient customs we believed in solely."
        But here's the reason why so many died:
        Our leaders failed to use ears, mouth and eyes.

Was it not always so? Don't *most* men live
in "quiet desperation," in some cave
that someone else provides or else their own?
Fame/power/glory/riches are a sieve.
To do the *right* thing well, in the *right* way
for purpose also *right*, this is, alone,
the course to satisfaction and self-worth.
"Each" is to blame. "Each" closes senses down–
plugs up his eyes with mud, his throat with sand.
No wonder modern life seems so perverse.
Not many *feel*; too many grope around.
Whatever we are serving, it's not Man.
    So here's my reason for what we've become:
    Men act like shadows when their senses numb.

You don't fool *me*. I see you walking in
and recognize you, after all these years.
I wonder if you recognize me, too,
and soon find out. A young enlisted man
struts out to me. Perhaps he's going to jeer.
But then he bows in public, in full view,
and puts an envelope inside my hat.
Then he salutes me! Must have come from you,
so I stand up, returning his salute.
He goes away. I look. It's money. What?
A hundred dollars. That's two hundred yen!
A month of food for families of my men.
     Since pity makes one poorer, I can see
     why you sent someone else so decently.

Well, I go home that day, well satisfied
because of your donation for my men–
the more so since, for once, I've more to show
than Precious Jade. But as I turn to go,
I see the same enlisted man. And when
I go a little slower, *he* goes slow.
If that's his game, no need to make it hard.
Duty is work enough. No playing games.
I walk back home and watch him stop outside,
write something down and check on it besides,
stopping a passer-by. To get my name?
Perhaps, although I'm not put on my guard.

    What does it matter? What could happen now?
    Assuming it once mattered anyhow.

The next week, after begging, I come home
to find your invitation at my door.
You ask us both to dinner. We're in rags.
What will we wear? But Precious Jade won't go.
She doesn't mix with others anymore.
Her face, you see. A knock, and then some wag
presents me with a package "from your tailor,
who much regrets not sending it before
although it has been paid for years ago."
A full-dress suit intended for a sailor!
An admiral, in fact. "It was the war
that kept us from delivering, you know."

     Another act of kindness to save face.
     You really know the customs of this place.

So I come here to see you. You're alone.
There's too much food. "My 'fridge is on the blink,"
you say to me; "please, won't you take some home?"
You reckon I won't take it, if I think
it's charity from you. Still saving face!
I'll take it, friend, for children of my men.
But *I'm* no longer worried by disgrace.
Thank you for being worried *for* me, Ben,
and asking for my story. Nice to know
you've been assigned to write the history
of all the battles in our late Great Show.
A better man to do it couldn't be.
        But now I've got to wonder, my good friend,
        why you're mixed up with those Tribunal men.

I think that your Tribunal's hunting *me*.
How clever of me, sitting in the street
right underneath their noses! What a treat
that, but for you, they might have known defeat.
I haven't *tried* to hide. I feel no "heat."
Whatever's yet to be, just let it be.
The men who were machine-gunned! Must be that.
The second boat was spared? Thank god, survivors.
The man with no arms lived? That's just amazing.
All massacres create their own insiders.
The winners do the damning or the praising.
But thank you, anyway, for this new hat.

    I wore these on my tunic, just for you –
    chrysanthemums – because you bought them new.

And now, my friend, you've got a new dilemma.
Your duty is to turn me in and write
endorsements for the War Court's fell decision.
My role's to be an object of derision,
whether guilty or not. Well, that's all right.
It doesn't matter much. This sailor fellow
no longer cares what happens to him now,
except for what it means to Precious Jade.
We're married. Thanks. I really had a time
obtaining her consent. "No way, no how."
She was ashamed, her spirit retrograde
as if it were *her* fault. That's the *real* crime.

    We had no one to go through, her or me.
    "I love you still," I said, "and not from pity."

Seeing I know that you're an academic,
pulled from reserves to write about this war,
I see a small dilemma. It's endemic.
Let's say you turn me in. You'll hear the roar
as they rip someone innocent apart.
If you *don't* turn me in – to serve the cause
that you were told to work on from the start,
Justice – you'll have to sacrifice your laws.
Serve Law and sacrifice what must be true,
or serve the Truth – as academics do –
and thumb your nose at Law. Conflicting duty!
I hope you work it out. This one's a beauty.

    I've got a feel for what you're going through,
    but no idea of what you're going to do.

Whichever way you go's all right with me,
so don't feel guilt about me, either way.
Fortunes of war. Or live another day.
It's all the same, when samurai are free.
Each day could be the last. I live to feel,
so I won't go down easy. Uncle said,
"Don't throw your life away. Too soon we're dead.
To struggle on is rare and yet more real."
Yes, living *is* the harder thing to do.
All lives are but a comment on that fact,
whether we face up bravely or defect.
My life has been that way. I *know* it's true.
      Please take these two insignia from me.
      Chrysanthemums. Your gift has set me free.

Ben, can you take a hint? This history
you have to write – *don't* try to tell the truth.
No one can know, in war, essential fact.
So make it fiction. This conceit could be
a clever means to cover what's uncouth
while shaking dust away for those who act
or feel or think, to read between the lines.
Be a one-sided jingo. Thump your drum.
Avoid explosive issues. Judge no men,
especially your bosses. Even then,
give all close calls to *your* side, since you won.
If you do this, you're sure to come out fine.

     In peacetime, Navy rules are not obscure.
     Suck up, and be an admiral for sure.

It's lightens me, by years, just talking here.
Remember how we toured in salad days?
You were my mirror image, in some ways:
a man who did his duty, with no fear.
Too bad good men are buried for their skills
by those less worthy, men who love control.
No matter what they say, say what they will,
there is no meritocracy at all.
Advancement is a scam, a happenstance,
that keeps us from determining how low
the values that we hold, by circumstance,
will be reduced, to ashes, as we go.

   It's time for *me* to go. I'll be at home,
   should any need me. Or come by alone.

A package with a memo, Jade. I'll read:
"Supreme Commander, Allied High Command.
To whom it may concern: Provide the bearer
passports for self and wife, as they may need,
and visas. Book passage out of Japan
for any time, from any place they care for,
by sea to France, Monaco. No return.
Pursuant to rule, Administration
deems this a hardship case. The man's a gambler,
unable to ply his trade. The woman's burned
and needs attention of skilled plastic surgeons.
Authenticate: through HQ: BN, handler."
    He's just like me, this old friend that I've found.
    A good man twists bureaucracy around.

A small enclosure: "To my gambler friend:
You see I've solved our problem. Hope that you
can learn to bluff again. To take out cash,
turn assets into U.S. bonds, and then
take down the numbers. Memorize them through,
then <u>burn</u> the bonds – <u>don't</u> throw them in the trash.
See Embassy in Paris for a refund.
You were right, about Dubuque. Reinvest
Toyota, Mitsubishi, or some other.
Your team will own the world before it's done.
You warned me, 'Keep an eye on island pests.'
'Trade's the equivalent of war,' now say your brothers.
  'They never learn,' you said. You're right, and wrong.
  'Never again' is now a marching song."

"Dear Former Captain: Thanks for what you did.
Except for radiation, Jade is cured.
Her face is back to normal. Even better,
she has no wrinkles! Read your <u>History</u>,
in all twelve volumes; mostly it's manure.
Seems you can take a hint, down to the letter!
Congratulations, getting your new flag
and for promotion back in academe.
You're good at bluffing, too, to win them both.
'Admiral Doctor Professor!' What a tag!
I make my living gambling. It's obscene.
Men drop their money on me. I'm not loath.
     I hold my own among square-headed men
     and make them <u>pay</u>. Eternally, your friend."

NOTES

Speech apocopates, depending on meter or vowels: An' (for "and"), adm'ral, brav'ry, diff'rent, emp'ror, every, fam'ly, gen'ral, -in' (for the suffix "-ing" sometimes), pow'r, pray'r, princip'ly, sev'ral, tem-per'ture or temp'rature, T'e'r del Fuego, trav'ling. "Going" can be one syllable, "goyne."

Page/Line.

7,6.   *SINECURES:* Pronounced, "SIN-uh-sures;" "land holdings," "keeps," "endowments."

7,12.   *ETA JIMA:* Site of Naval Academy.

12,12. *BANZAI:* "Hurrah."

54,7.   *XO:* "Executive Officer."

57,11. *RIDE TO THE SOUND OF THE GUNS:* Gen. George Custer's favorite motto, said once too often.

70.13. *C-IN-C:* "Commander-in-Chief."

79,4.   *CO:* "Commanding Officer."

89,14. *TINTINNABULATION:* Percussing bells; *hence,* "confusion."

92,12. *SAKE:* Rice wine.

101,6. *TWENTY-FIVE:* Knots.

109,14. *BUSHIDO:* Japanese military values; the way of the warrior.

111,14. The important question is not whether the Emperor was forced to ride his horse, but how he managed to stay seated.

117,8. *HECTARES:* Like acres, but 2.7 more of them.

124,1. *BROAD ISLAND:* Literal translation of "Hiroshima."

149,12. *HQ:* "Headquarters."

(James Sutton may be contacted by e-mail at JamesSutton@Juno.com.)